Jack Stories

Favorite Memories
of
Jack Jordan Ammann Jr

Compiled and Edited
by Lillie Ammann

Jack Stories

Favorite Memories of Jack Jordan Ammann Jr

© 2012 Lillian A. Ammann

Lillie's Lovely Little Publishing Company

603 Mauze Dr

San Antonio, TX 78216

210-344-5554

lillie@lillieammann.com

www.lillieammann.com

and

www.lillieammann.net

ISBN: 978-0-9665912-4-8

Dedicated to God—Father, Son, and Holy Ghost

In loving memory of

Jack Jordan Ammann Jr

1933 – 2012

To Pierre,
Thank you for
making our shopping
trips fun. Jack always
loved to talk to you.
Julie
Ammann

Contents

Introduction

For years I encouraged Jack to write his stories, but he preferred to tell them—over and over again! I occasionally wrote a blog post about Jack, perhaps including one or more of his favorite stories.

On the morning that he died, the house soon filled with family and friends. We sat around his bed telling "Jack stories." I had always known Jack was a very special man—a remarkable character, but I realize I am just a tiny bit biased. Hearing the memories others shared about Jack, I realized he had touched many lives and left a legacy of love, laughter, and inspiration that should be shared.

Family and friends who came to the visitation or the reception after the funeral were invited to write favorite memories of Jack on the index cards provided. I contacted others who had stories to share and prayed I didn't overlook anyone. Thank you to each person who contributed to this book and to each person who touched Jack's life. I value you and your memories.

I hope this collection of memories, anecdotes, and tributes will bring you happy memories, inspiration, and laughter, as Jack did in person throughout his life.

Lillian A (Lillie) Ammann
Jack's wife

A Jack by Any Other Name

Jack liked to use his full name: Jack Jordan Ammann Jr. But to his family he was always "Jackie" as he was called in childhood. He also identified himself in other ways, depending on the circumstances. Since he always wore an Aggie tee-shirt, if he called someone who might not immediately recognize his name, he would identify himself as "Aggie Jack." When Lillie owned the interior landscape company, Jack handled the accounts payable and receivable. Whenever he talked to a vendor or a customer, he identified himself as "Jack Ammann, Mr. Lillie." After Lillie sold the plant company and became a freelance writer and editor, Jack introduced himself to her clients as "Mr. Lillie."

Jack's Stories

Stories Jack Told Often

The following stories are ones Jack told often.

However, they are written in third person with no attempt to quote Jack exactly.

The Insane Asylum

Jack loved to tell people he was born at the insane asylum. His grandparents worked at the San Antonio State Hospital, called the insane asylum in those days before political correctness. His mother went into labor while visiting her parents, and the hospital doctor delivered Jack at the state hospital.

One of his favorite jokes was about a man who was changing a tire on his car beside the road outside the state hospital. Patients were hanging on the fence, staring out at the world beyond the hospital. The motorist was having trouble getting the lug nuts loose, and one of the patients called out, "You're turning them the wrong way." The man changed direction and the lug nuts came loose immediately. He asked the patient who had pointed out his problem, "How did you know what I was doing wrong?" The patient answered, "We're crazy in here—not stupid."

Baby Jackie with his mother

Young Patriot

Jack developed a strong sense of patriotism at a very young age. During World War II, he took part of his lunch money to buy war stamps, and when he had accumulated enough stamps, he bought war bonds.

He regularly pulled his little red wagon throughout the neighborhood to pick up scrap metal to contribute to the war cause. The fire station was the collection point, and the firemen got to know him very well. One of them would see him coming down the sidewalk and say, "Here comes Jackie with another wagon full of scrap metal."

As the country engaged in other conflicts in the later years of his life, Jack always bemoaned the fact that civilians didn't pull together to help in the war effort as people did back in his childhood during World War II.

The young patriot with his mother,
Louise Mangham

Wedding Cakes and Bouncing Tires Don't Mix

Jack's maternal grandmother, Emma Mangham, owned the Manor Tea Room and made a lot of wedding cakes. As a teenager, Jack made deliveries for her. On one occasion, Jack carried the large and beautiful wedding cake down the steps from the tea room to street level. He sat the cake on the sidewalk between the rock retaining wall and the street. He removed the spare tire so he had enough room in the trunk for the cake. He tossed the tire over the retaining wall onto the lawn in front of the building. The tire bounced on the lawn and back down onto the sidewalk—right in the middle of the cake! Although Jack was terrified to admit to his grandmother what he had done, she told him not to worry. She could fix the problem and no one would ever be able to tell anything had happened. She went to the freezer and took out several layers of cake. Then she cut the damaged part out of the cake and replaced it with the frozen cake. She frosted the cake and added the decorations and voilà, a beautiful wedding cake. The frozen pieces would thaw by the time the cake was served, and no one knew that a few hours before, the cake had been smashed by a bouncing tire.

Jack with his grandmother, Emma Mangham, many years after the cake episode

Interrupted Education

During his fourth year of college, Jack received a notification of a change in his draft status to 1A—eligible for the draft with no more student deferment. He called the draft board and explained he was in a five-year degree plan, but he was told, "We gave you four years to get your degree. Now it's time to serve your country."

Jack decided to enlist rather than wait to be drafted. Although he had to spend three years instead of two, he would be able to choose the kind of work he did. He had worked some for his father, who owned a photogrammetric mapping business, so he signed up to be a stereoscope map compiler.

His first year in the Army was easy for him—he was in training the entire time, and he already knew how to do the job. After training, there were only three locations he could be assigned: San Francisco, Heidelberg, or Tokyo. He spent one year at The Presidio in San Francisco, California. While he was there, he served as a lay reader at the Episcopal Cathedral there.

He spent his final year in the Army in Heidelberg, Germany. He had carried over thirty days of leave and accumulated another thirty days in Germany. He and a buddy took a two month tour of Europe. His buddy had the car, and Jack bought the gas. They visited several countries and saw a number of exciting sites, including St. John's Basilica in Rome and the site in Austria where the winter Olympics were held. By the end of the trip, though, they were running short of money. They drove by a huge field full of ripe cabbages and decided this was the answer to their concerns about not having anything to eat. They climbed the fence into the field and gathered heads of cabbage. They had plenty to eat—as long as they wanted raw cabbage.

KP Duty and Guard Duty

In the Army, Jack took any job he was assigned seriously and performed it to be the best of his ability, just as he did with every civilian job he held throughout his life. As a private, he had to perform KP duty. After spending hours washing piles of dirty, greasy pots and pans, he vowed he'd find an easier way. Detergent had just been introduced on the market, but the Army was using old-fashioned soap. So Jack went to the Post Exchange and bought the largest container of dish detergent he could find. The next time he had to perform KP duty, he took his bottle of detergent and had the dirty pots sparkling in much less time than he had spent before. The sergeant in charge of the kitchen wanted to know how he managed to do such a good job in such a short time. Jack showed him the bottle of detergent, but when the sergeant asked him to leave it for others to use, Jack said the Army would have to buy its own detergent. The sergeant did buy the detergent, making life easier for every soldier who pulled KP duty.

The soldiers rotated as guards on the front gate to the post. The mess hall provided a sack lunch for the night guards. When Jack picked up his sack lunch on the way to guard duty one night, he looked in the bag and found a cheese sandwich—made up of one slice of cheese and two slices of bread. No mayonnaise or mustard, no lettuce or tomatoes, nothing but cheese and dry bread. The sergeant saw what he had, grabbed it from him, and threw it against the wall. Then he told the private who had prepared the lunch to start over and this time do it right. Jack walked out of the kitchen with a ham and cheese sandwich, with mustard, lettuce, and tomatoes, and a piece of fruit. Guards never got cheese-on-dry-bread sack lunches again.

Late one night, Jack was on guard duty, and a sergeant returned to the post after a night on the town, staggering around like he was drunk. Jack asked him for his ID. The sergeant became belligerent and said he didn't have to tell any private who he was. Jack said anyone coming through that gate, even the commander, was required to identify himself and show credentials to verify he was authorized to be on the post. The inebriated sergeant said he didn't have to show an ID, and he wasn't going to do it. Jack called for the captain of the guard in a nearby building. Then he raised his weapon, chambered a round, and demanded again that the sergeant show his ID. The sergeant said, "Aw, you wouldn't dare shoot me." Jack said, "I'll shoot you and sit down on the curb and eat my sandwich." By this time the captain of the guard and two more guards had arrived to arrest the sergeant. Jack learned later that he had to serve time in the post jail and was punished with a reduction in rank.

Highest Paid Engineer

After his three-year Army enlistment, Jack returned to Texas A&M to finish his education. Near the end of his senior year, he was interviewed by recruiters from several different companies. One of the recruiters told him they couldn't consider him because they were hiring only students who had a B average. Jack said, "You just told me you were going to the University of Texas next, right?" The recruiter acknowledged that he was. Jack said, "Well, a B average at Texas is a numerical grade of 80 to 90. Here at A&M, a B is 84 to 92. I have an 80 average, which is a C here but would be a B at Texas." The recruiter admitted he didn't know that and agreed to consider Jack for the position.

He was invited to go to Dayton, Ohio, to interview. He didn't have any money to make the trip, so he borrowed from the Association of Former Students. Frigidaire Division of General Motors had a room reserved for him at a very nice hotel, and the company sent a car to take him to the plant. When he arrived at the plant, he was escorted to an accounting office, where he was given a check to cover his travel, hotel, and meal expenses. Then he was taken on a tour of the plant and was interviewed by managers in several different departments. At the end of the day, the human resources manager offered him a job at the pay of $551.67 per month, which was more than the normal pay for beginning engineers. Wanting to appear cool, Jack asked if he could have a few days to think it over. He already knew he would accept the job but waited to make it official until he had been home a couple of days.

He was very proud of the fact he was the highest paid engineer in his graduating class. The next highest paid person was a graduate with a double major, and he was paid $550.00. That $1.67 more per month that Jack made was always a bragging point for him.

Highest Efficiency Rating

Jack was a first-line foreman at Frigidaire Division of General Motors in a department in which all the supervisors were industrial engineers. He worked the night shift producing refrigerator parts. One night, he had a work order to produce 200 refrigerator backs and sides for a particular model. As was normally done, his team set up the line and ran a test part. An outside inspector examined it and agreed everything was correct, so they ran the entire order. Only then did the inspector check again and discover the sides and backs that were produced were for the wrong model. There was an extra hole not needed in the part they were supposed to produce. Jack called his boss and asked what to do. The boss authorized overtime to run the correct parts and told Jack to send the 200 sides and backs to the baler to be destroyed because the model year was coming to an end.

Although Jack usually followed orders exactly, this time he couldn't bring himself to throw away newly produced parts. So he had his forklift operator move some things in their storage area and put the parts there. A few weeks later, he was given a work order to produce 200 sides and backs for refrigerators to be shipped to Canada—the model that he had been told to destroy. In about fifteen minutes, the forklift operator had moved the hidden parts out. Jack called his boss and told him they were through with the work order—what should they do now? As a result, Jack's section had the highest efficiency rating, not only for Frigidaire, but for all of General Motors. All because Jack couldn't stand to let something go to waste.

When people from other departments asked Jack how he managed to achieve such a high efficiency rating, he answered, "I could tell you, but then I'd have to kill you." Only his direct supervisor knew what had transpired.

Corvette

When Jack was working for Frigidaire Division of General Motors, Chevrolet introduced the Corvette Stingray. Jack saw one in a dealership on the way to work, and when he arrived, he told the plant manager, "Boss, I think I have to have one of those Corvettes." "You want one? Come on up to my office." The plant manager called his counterpart at the Chevrolet assembly plant and said, "One of my boys wants one of your cars." The Chevrolet manager said they had just completed a Corvette run, and it would be several weeks before they did another run.

Jack's boss explained that when a General Motors member of management bought a General Motors car, they took every option available. Jack placed the order, and the plant manager contacted the General Motors financing department and arranged financing. Arrangements were made to deliver the car to a dealership in a small town near Dayton. About a month later, Jack went to the dealership to check on the status of the car. The dealership had his car on display in the showroom. They had never had a Corvette at that dealership, and they wanted to show it off a little before they notified Jack it was in.

After Jack got the car, the plant manager asked him where he was going to park it. Jack said he parked in the employee parking lot. The plant manager said, "My wife has a covered reserved parking spot next to mine. She never uses it, so you can park your Corvette there." So not only did Jack have the best car among Frigidaire employees, he also had the best parking space—right next to the plant manager.

Home to Texas

Jack liked his job at Frigidaire, but he realized, "You can take the boy out of Texas, but you can't take Texas out of the boy." He found a job at Kelly Air Force Base, but he told the hiring manager he had to give Frigidaire all the notice they needed. Kelly agreed to give him as much time as he needed—they appreciated that he was the kind of employee who would not leave an employer in a difficult situation.

When Jack told his bosses at Frigidaire he was leaving, they were very disappointed because he was such a good foreman. However, they really appreciated the amount of notice and Jack's willingness to train his replacement before he left.

Several weeks later, after the new foreman was ready to take over the job, Jack left the snow and ice of Ohio and returned to sunny south Texas.

Jack with his Corvette

For Lack of a Bearing

When Kelly Air Force Base was assigned the responsibility for the overhaul of the C-5, Jack became the project engineer. The first overhaul job was expected to be a big event. The colonel and all the civilian managers planned to be there when the first engine came off the overhaul line. However, when the workers put the engine on the balancing machine, the machine didn't work, and the production show didn't happen. The problem turned out to be a defective bearing in the machine.

Jack called the manufacturer of the balancing machine and spoke to someone in management. He explained it was critical to get the machine back on line immediately if not sooner. The company representative made the arrangements and called Jack back. "The bearing will be on Eastern Jet Freight arriving at the San Antonio Airport at 4:30 AM tomorrow." Jack was at the airport at 4:30 the next morning. He picked up the package, delivered it to Kelly, and instructed the third shift maintenance crew to replace the defective bearing.

When the colonel and civilian management arrived at work at 8:00 AM, they came to see if any progress had been made on solving the problem. They were amazed to learn that the bearing had been replaced, the machine was operating fine, and the first engine was in overhaul and would be coming off the line very soon.

Jack gave his standard answer to the question of how he had accomplished this: "I could tell you, but then I'd have to kill you."

Dream Home

After several years of apartment living, Jack was ready for a house. He contracted with his uncle, Tom McNeil, who was a builder, to build the house. Tom's architect drew up the plans and showed them to Jack. Jack really liked the front elevation and the size and shape of the building. However, the inside layout wasn't what he had in mind. So he took his art gum eraser and erased everything inside the exterior walls. He sketched out the layout he wanted and handed it back to the architect for the design to be drafted again with the layout Jack designed. He included some unusual features in the house, including a rock fireplace in the living room, the other side of which is a barbecue grill in the kitchen, a rock wall in the bedroom, and a short rock wall between the living room and the den.

He went to the bank (San Antonio Savings Association, long defunct) and asked to be named the general contractor on the loan so that he determined when the work was satisfactory for payments at various increments. He visited the job site every day after work to make sure everything was done to his satisfaction. The first day the rock was being applied to the exterior, the stonemason had put the mortar to the outside face of the rock. Jack explained that the rock was supposed to be exposed and stand out from the mortar. Fortunately the mortar hadn't completely dried, so the stonemason could scrape out the excess.

Jack was so proud of his home and loved to show it off and tell visitors how he designed and had it built.

He lived in the house for a couple of years before he met Lillie. In later years, though, he always said he built the house to be a home for Lillie and him to live in throughout their lives. When Lillie reminded him he didn't even know her until years after he built the house, he always responded, "But God knew."

Hurry to Buy Before the Price Goes Down

Throughout school, at Frigidaire, and in the early days at Kelly Air Force Base, Jack used a slide rule for complicated calculations. In the 1970s, Texas Instruments came out with the first calculator that would perform slide rule functions. One of the engineers who worked in Jack's office bought one of the very first ones on the market. Of course, Jack had to get his right away. He took vacation time and drove from Kelly to Joske's in downtown San Antonio to buy himself a calculator. He was pleased to discover that the price had been lowered since his coworker bought his the day before. Soon all the engineers wanted to have their own slide rule calculator. The price seemed to go down with every purchase, so Jack started telling others, "You'd better hurry and get yours before the price goes down."

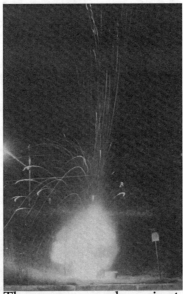

The cannon made a giant firecracker on the Fourth of July

The Cannon

Jack and his friend Leonard Specht decided it would be fun to build a cannon. They designed a working model of a Civil War siege mortar perfectly to scale. They took the plans to a machinist, who built the cannon to their specifications. The place where the cannon was built was a rather isolated area, and Jack, Specht, and the machinist were all eager to see if the cannon worked as it was supposed to. So they set the cannon out in the parking lot a good way from the building, which had a row of windows all around the perimeter. They added black powder and lit the wick. The explosion was so powerful it broke every single window in the building. They all agreed it worked just fine!

Several years later, during Lillie's last year of college, a campus organization (Gamma Delta Iota) planned a float for the Homecoming Parade. The Southwestern University baseball and basketball teams were the Pirates, so the float had a pirate theme. Jack took the cannon to Georgetown, and their friend, Phil Huth, dressed as a pirate on the float, was designated to set off the cannon when the float passed the judging stand. Phil lit the wick, but nothing happened immediately. He looked down into the barrel just at the moment of explosion. His face and arms were peppered with tiny bits of gravel and rock. Fortunately, he wasn't seriously injured, but he was uncomfortable and looked awful for a few weeks. Unfortunately, a couple of years later, Phil stepped on a landmine in the Vietnam War and was killed.

Cherry Tomatoes and The Celebrity

Jack and Lillie were returning home from a trip. Back in those days, airlines served real meals on long trips. The lunch included a salad with a cherry tomato. When Jack bit into the tomato, he didn't have his mouth completely closed. Tomato juice and seeds spattered all over the hair of the woman in the row in front of them. The blonde hair was in a bouffant style with lots of hair spray. When the plane arrived in San Antonio, Jack and Lillie were the last to deplane. They stepped off the plane to discover the Chamber of Commerce was providing a red carpet welcome for a lady with blonde bouffant hair … sprinkled with tomato seeds! It was Betsy Palmer, at that time appearing on the TV show *What's My Line*. They never learned why she was riding in coach, but they suspected she always went first class after that trip!

Jack and Lillie on a
trip

Tabled

Lillie started making terrariums and growing African violets as a hobby, but it didn't take long for the hobby to grow into a business—a small plant store in Artisans' Alley. At the time, a nursery license cost about $30 per year. The large nursery businesses wanted to eliminate the competition from small shops and from hobby growers. A nursery trade association lobbied the state legislature to raise the price of a nursery license to several hundred dollars. Their rationale was that some people acquired a nursery license only so they could buy plants and gardening supplies wholesale. While there was probably some abuse of the system in this way, there were many small businesses and hobbyists who sold plants—but nowhere near enough to pay several hundred dollars a year for a license. Hobby clubs for growers of a variety of plants—African violets, bromeliads, cactus, orchids, and more—often held shows that included sales by individual members.

Lillie was a member of the Magic Knight African Violet Society, and the members made a trip to lobby the committee considering the bill. The group asked Jack to be its spokesman, and he was reviewing the points of his presentation with club members in the hallway before the meeting began. Others heard him speaking and asked him to represent their group as well. When it was his turn to address the committee, he began, "My name is Jack Ammann. I am here to represent the three members of the Exotic Orchid Club, the ten members of the Village Cactus Society, the twenty-seven members of the Bromeliad Hobbyists, the fifty-nine members of the Magic Knight African Violet Club, the four hundred members of the North Texas Bromeliad Growers, the seven hundred members of the Indoor Plant Society, and the five thousand members of the Herb Growers of Texas."

He then explained how each of these organizations held periodic sales so the members could find new homes for the plants they propagated and earn a little money to support their hobby. After he concluded his presentation, the chairman looked at the committee members one by one. "I think we can agree to table this bill indefinitely, can't we?" Everyone nodded in agreement ... and the price of a nursery license in the state of Texas remained affordable for hobby growers and small businesses.

Jack and Lillie
dressed to impress

Stop the War on Women

Jack hated domestic violence or any mistreatment of women and children. When he was a deputy constable, he sometimes worked security at private businesses.

On one such occasion, he was in the parking lot of a bar near closing time, and he saw a man hitting a woman in the face with his fist. Jack ran over, pulled his police flashlight out of his belt, and brought it down on the upraised arm of the man preparing to punch the woman again. The flashlight was so heavy and Jack used so much force that the man's arm was broken. He had to be taken for medical treatment before he was taken to jail.

When Jack told Lillie about it, she said, "It's a wonder you didn't get accused of police brutality." Jack answered, "It would be worth it to keep that woman from being hurt any more."

Stealing is Theft

On his lunch break one day when Jack was working as a deputy constable, he had finished his meal and was looking around the restaurant as he drank the rest of his tea. He noticed the group at a nearby table leaving several dollar bills on the table for the tip. Shortly after they left, the bus boy came over to clean the table. As he wiped the surface, he slipped several of the bills off the table into his pocket. The waitress might think the group left a paltry tip, but no one would know that half of the generous tip was now in the bus boy's apron. At least, that's what the bus boy must have thought. When Jack saw the boy pocket the cash, he got up, handcuffed the young man, read him his rights, and took him to jail. The bus boy didn't think taking a few dollars was a big deal, but to Jack stealing is stealing, no matter the size of the theft.

After that, whenever he ate in a restaurant, Jack made a point to hand the tip directly to the wait person. He would track the server down on the other side of the restaurant, if necessary, to be sure the tip money went into the waiter's hand and nowhere else.

Racing a Plane to California

One year, Jack and Lillie and their friends Ken and Grace Anne Schaefer were involved in network marketing with Rexall. Grace Anne and Lillie were both aspiring writers and members of the Romance Writers of America (RWA). RWA had a large conference scheduled in Anaheim, California, and Rexall had its big convention in Long Beach the following week.

Grace Anne and Lillie flew to California for the RWA event, then spent a few days in a Motel 6 in Long Beach until time for the Rexall conference. They all stayed at Motel 6 for less than one night at the ritzy hotel and had more fun. All four had round-trip tickets on USAir. However, USAir had recently had at least one major crash and several near-misses and maintenance problems. Jack decided he would not set foot on a USAir plane. So when it came time to make the trip, he left in his car a couple of days before Ken left on the airplane.

Jack liked to tell people that he drove all the way with the cruise control on his Chevrolet Impala set at 125 and arrived just in time to pick Ken up at the airport before meeting Grace Anne and Lillie at the Motel 6.

On the return trip, Grace Anne and Ken used their airplane tickets, but Lillie rode home in the car with Jack. They hoped USAir used the money they made from the nonrefundable tickets to improve the maintenance on their airplanes!

This is also where Jack's being a kid at heart got another little boy in trouble. They were having lunch in the grand, if somewhat shabby, restaurant of the Queen Mary when a delightful little boy about four years old began playing peek-a-boo with Jack over the back of his chair. As the meal progressed, the child would make faces and sneak peeks while his mother ate her lunch. Then mischief got the best of

Jack, and he stuck his tongue out at the little boy who made a shocked face. A few minutes later on his next peek, the child stuck his tongue out at Jack. Unfortunately that was the time his mother had turned to see what he was doing. She soundly scolded him, and Jack protested that it was his fault because he stuck his tongue out first, and she should scold him. The mother told Jack the boy knew better than to behave so rudely, and her look and tone made it plain she was scolding Jack. Jack was chagrined and made no further attempts to engage the child in games.

Jack and Lillie
with
Ken and Grace Anne
on California trip

Divine Interference

Jack was not a regular church-goer, but he had a strong faith. He often spoke of the divine guidance he had received in his life. He didn't regret anything that had happened or any decisions he had made because everything led to putting him in a place to meet Lillie.

He felt it was divine intervention that gave him the desire to come back to Texas from Ohio and that provided a job he loved at Kelly Air Force. He was sure it was divine intervention that placed Lillie in the same department he was in when she got a summer job at Kelly.

He believed many other things that happened in his life came from divine intervention.

However in the last couple of years of his life, he often confused words. He never lost his faith that God gave him all the good things he received in his life, but he started calling it "divine interference."

Some of Jack's Favorite and Famous Sayings

Friendship:

"A friend is someone who would take a bullet for you; everyone else is just an acquaintance."

Lillie says: "I can't say they would all take a bullet for him, but Jack had many very good friends—as the stories in this book demonstrate."

Business:

"I do business with people, not with companies."

When shopping in a place where he hadn't already established relationships with people and where he found the service lacking:

"Good help is hard to find."

"I hate to have a hard time spending my money."

Work:

"Work smarter, not harder."

"I can do more on the way back and forth to the restroom than most people do when they're working."

Communication:

"There are two parts to communication: the speaker has to deliver the message and the listener has to understand it."

About Someone Who Talked A Lot:

"He sounds like he was vaccinated with a Victrola needle."

Politics:

"I sit to the right of Attila the Hun."

Education:

"College doesn't make you a fountain of information; it just teaches you how to find the information."

Lillie says: "That was before the Internet and Google."

Accomplishment:

"The improbable can be done immediately, but the impossible takes just a little bit longer."

"Eliminate the word *cannot* from your vocabulary."

Taking Action:

"It's easier to ask forgiveness than to ask permission."

Assume:

"Don't assume. It makes an ass out of you and me."

Approval:

"He/she is a scholar and knightly gentleman/gentlewoman."

"I love a gal/guy with a sense of humor."

"It's jam up and jelly roll."

Fear:

"{Whatever} scared me to death, and I'm fearless."

Less than Perfection:

"It's close enough for government work."

Aging:

"Getting old is better than the alternative."

Lillie says: "I don't think Jack believes this any longer. Read the last page of this book to see what he thinks about the *alternative* now."

Lillie and Jack early in married life

Jack's beloved dream home

Jack Stories

Favorite Stories from
Jack's Family and Friends

The stories are printed as the authors wrote them,

with only minor editing to correct errors and to maintain consistency.

The order of quotes is completely random.

A Class Act

One memory that sticks out in my mind is one time we all went to Goerke's for dinner. Pam's nephew Brian, who was five or six years old at the time, ran into the parking lot and fell down. Jack ran to him and picked him up and hugged him close. By the time Pam got there, Brian was fine. Pam really appreciated Jack's concern and care.

Jack was such a class act. He described Pam as a "most gracious lady." That meant a lot to me.

Jack always helped me out—always backed me up. When I decided to try for an Extra class amateur radio license, some of my friends discouraged me, but Jack encouraged me. I didn't have as much education as Jack did, but he always took up for me. He was always an inspiration.

Thomas (Tommy) Truehardt
Friend
Tommy and Jack were radio buddies and Lillie and Pam were African violet friends for some time before they discovered that the radio buddies were married to the African violet friends.

A Great Person

Jack was a great person, always joking and thinking of others. Charlie loved him dearly and loved being around him. I will miss him very much. God bless and keep him in His hands.

Pat Ammann
Jack's aunt, widow of Charles Ammann

Happy Jack

Mean as Hell

I had seen Jack when I was a teenager hanging around the area where local hot rodders went to race. I didn't know him, but I saw him frequently, and he was the one who would warn us when the police were coming so we could leave before they got there.

However, the first time I actually met Jack was when I was working at Tom Benson Honda Mazda. He brought one of his Mazdas in for some work, and he hung over the car watching everything I did and telling me how to do it. After I finished, I told Frank Arocha, the mechanic I worked with, that Jack was mean as hell and mad at me the whole time. Frank told me Jack wasn't mad—that was just the way he acted—and once I got to know him, I'd learn he was very nice. Over time, I did get to know Jack and discover his true personality for myself.

When I worked at a garage off San Pedro, my coworker Rick thought his Mustang was the fastest car on the road. I told him there were a couple of Mazdas around town that were faster than his car. Rick said, "There ain't no way a couple of little rice burners can beat this car." I called Jack without anyone knowing it, and he came over right away. When he drove up in front of the building, I acted like it was a coincidence that he showed up then. He got out of the car, dressed in shorts, Aggie T-shirt, and shoes with socks. He looked like a poor, old man. The guys were talking among themselves saying the race was going to be embarrassing for Jack. Rick said, "You mean I'm going to race that old man?" I said I was willing to bet $50, and Rick took me up on it. We got someone to hold the money, and the two racers drove to a nearby parking lot. When the light changed, they took off, and Jack just blew the Mustang away. It wasn't even close. No one could believe that little blue Mazda driven by that "old man" could beat a Mustang driven by a young, macho man.

Mike at the body shop was building a Mustang. He didn't like Rick, and he was determined to outdo Rick. He said, "You know the little Mazda beat the hell out of that other Mustang, but it's not going to happen to me. I'll beat that little blue car so bad it's going to shut down all the talk about fast cars, and it will prove Rick doesn't know what he's doing." I called Jack and told him about Mike's challenge. Jack asked me what the car looked like. He could tell by the suspension whether the car could launch fast or not. I told him the suspension on this Mustang looked just like the one on Rick's car. So Jack showed up prepared to win big. Just like the race with Rick, this one wasn't even close. Jack was at the finish before Mike got a good start. All the bragging talk about fast cars was shut down, but not in the way Mike expected.

I asked Jack if it bothered him when people made jokes about A&M. He said it didn't—as long as he could make jokes about their schools. We knew a pharmacist named Joel, who was very smart and who had gone to the University of Texas. I told him that Jack was the smartest man I knew. He could figure out things like how many shoeboxes would fit in a room. And he did it without a calculator—just a pencil and a piece of paper. Jack always knew how to figure out a problem himself or find someone who could do it. He would never back down from a problem. Sometimes I'd want to give up, but Jack would never quit. Joel was offended that I said Jack was the smartest man I knew; Joel thought he was the smartest. I told him he was the second smartest, but he couldn't compete with an Aggie.

One time Jack was at the shop when I needed to deliver a vehicle to a customer. I asked him if he would follow me to the customer's house and bring me back to the shop. Of course, he agreed. Jack never said, "No." If you asked him to do something, he would do it. After we dropped the car off, we went down IH10 headed back to the shop on Fredericksburg Road. Jack asked me if I would like a course in high speed pursuit. In his law enforcement training, he had a course in high speed pursuit, and he wanted to show me how it was done. He was driving very fast and zigzagging in and out among the other cars on the highway, and I was just holding on until the course ended.

When he was a deputy constable, Jack helped with speeding stops. Someone would man the radar gun in a marked car, and Jack would pursue the speeders in Ole Blue Mazda—a hot rod out catching speeders.

On our deer hunting trips to Castroville, Jack would drive his Cadillac 90 mph on IH10, but in the Cadillac, it didn't feel like we were going that fast. I was afraid of wild hogs crossing the roadway—if we hit one of them, we'd be goners. Jack said there wasn't any danger of that.

He got up to 115 mph—the fastest I've ever gone. I was a nervous wreck holding on. Jack asked if I was scared, and I said, "No." No one wanted to let Jack know they were scared of his speed. He said the salesman told him that if the Cadillac didn't do 150 mph to bring it back and they would get one that did. Jack said he never took it up to 150 mph— he got it up to 148 mph and figured if it would go that fast, it would go 150.

Jack always said if we ever got pulled over to let him do the talking. He had so many contacts that he always seemed to have someone to call on for a favor. Even if he didn't know anyone, he managed to get acquainted with someone and persuade them to do whatever it was that he wanted done.

Jack could carry on a conversation with someone with a sixth grade education as well as with a college professor.

Jack Stories

It really burned him when he saw someone trying to make someone else look stupid. He would get into the conversation and show up the guy acting smart. He could talk more intelligently and use more and bigger words than the guy who was showing off.

Another thing that really offended him was men wearing hats or caps inside. If we went into a restaurant and saw men wearing hats, he would say loudly enough for them to hear, "Real men uncover when they come inside." He learned that at A&M, and he took it seriously all his life.

Jack was a real perfectionist, and he wanted everything done is a certain way. I'd be watching him do something, and he would say, "That's the OCD kicking in." He may not have been officially diagnosed with obsessive-compulsive disorder, but he could sure be obsessive and compulsive.

On one hunting trip, we had gone into Castroville for dinner. When we were going back to the hunting camp, we saw a little kitty that had apparently been abandoned by someone. He was in a tree near the gate, and he tried to get away from us. But the tree was growing kind of sideways and low to the ground, so Jack managed to catch him. Jack took that dirty, smelly kitty back to the camp house and fed him. When we headed back to San Antonio, Jack put the kitten in the car. The kitty climbed up on Jack's shoulders and wrapped himself around Jack's neck for the ride home. I understand that Jack had that kitty for many years until the cat died a few months before Jack did.

Anthony Friedrich
Friend/hunting buddy/mechanic

Grateful

Mr. Ammann was always so grateful to the staff when leaving the office. When we would call him in to the exam, he would say, "I'm coming at a high rate of speed!" He always made sure to thank the staff for the care given to him. Sometimes he would joke with me and pretend that his INR checks (finger pricks) were painful, but he was only kidding. I enjoyed hearing him talk about anything. Very wise man.

Vicky
Medical Assistant at Health Texas Medical Group, Blanco Rd.

The Hated "Pee Pills"

One day Jack and Lillie invited me to lunch. When they picked me up, Jack jokingly said, "You're paying, right?" I said, "Of course; I have your credit card." Jack chuckled and said, "I love a gal with a sense of humor!"

I would give Jack his medicine and would have to talk him into taking his "pee pills" (diuretics). On a good day, I would get him to take one. He was supposed to take four. His legs got really swollen, and he needed to take more "pee pills." I told him he had to take two, and he negotiated for one. I countered with four, and we finally settled on two.

The first time I came to their house, Lillie was making toast for Jack, and she burned it to a crisp. I thought to myself, "Wow! He must really love her to eat burnt toast without complaining." Later, they asked me to make Jack some toast. When I took him beautiful, evenly browned toast, he said, "That's just warm bread. Take it back and burn it." Even though eating burnt toast wasn't the sign of love I first thought, I learned that Jack really did love Lillie as much as I first thought.

In the hospital, Jack was going in and out of sleep. Every now and then he would wake up and call for Lillie just to tell her "I love you." I thought that was the sweetest thing!

Betsy Gonzales
Jack's caregiver and surrogate granddaughter

Wonderful Last Memory

Jack's favorite joke: Lillie and I would be working in her office, and Jack would come over to investigate. When he stuck his head in the door, I would say, "Hi, Jack," and he always responded, "Don't say that in an airport." Ha! Ha!

The last visit: My last visit with Jack was on a really good day. He was sitting in the den, and I sat with him awhile. He was so sweet and told me that Lillie was very lucky to have found me. I told him that I thought it was the other way around. What a wonderful last memory of him!

With love,
Jan McClintock
Friend/Lillie's editorial assistant and web designer

Jump!

I have many Jack stories—one of my favorites was the first time we met. Jack brought Lillian to visit me at my mom's in the summer of 1965. I was upset they were "late" (took about three hours to get to Leander), and I didn't make him welcome. I opened the door, hugged Lil, and said, "Jack, you don't want to come in, do you?" He said, "Yes, thank you." He visited with my mom and grandmother for about four hours, becoming friends with both of them, and my mom helped vouch for him with Lillie's parents.

When our daughter Anja was about five, we celebrated our wedding anniversary with a weekend at Jack and Lillie's. Anja was a bright child, and Jack enjoyed gently teasing her and talking to her. Jack and Lillie took us to a fancy restaurant, which I believe was called Mike and Charlie's. Our dinner was delicious and elegant, and Anja was a model of decorum. Jack wanted to impress her even more, so he ordered Bananas Foster prepared at the table. The chef put on quite a show and played almost directly to Anja, who watched in rapt delight. He served her dessert (vanilla ice cream with fried bananas) with a flourish. Anja smiled sweetly and proceeded to scrape the bananas off her ice cream. Jack pretended horror and admonished her for her super expensive scoop of vanilla ice cream. She smiled sweetly and announced, "I don't like bananas." End of discussion.

I always felt that my mother, grandmother, and I were at least in part responsible for Jack and Lillie's romance. Jack was always a memorable character, and he had a kind of bond with my grandmother whom everyone called Nannie. She was already kind of old when they met, and she wasn't always politically correct. One time Jack was in Mexico or somewhere on a ham radio trip, and he called her on a "patch." The man in Austin was explaining who Jack was, and she interrupted with, "I know who he is. He's that little fat man who married Lillian." More than twenty-five years later, Jack and Lillie were helping celebrate our Silver Wedding Anniversary, and they visited Nannie in a nursing home. When Jack walked in she greeted him as "that little fat man who married Lillian." She loved him and he loved her.

Another favorite memory and example of Jack's kind sense of humor: I had a mastectomy many years ago, and the first time I saw him afterwards with a fake boob, he stared intently at my chest, looking back and forth. Then he said, "Jump," causing me to laugh when he guessed correctly because the fake one didn't bounce.

Grace Anne Schaefer
Friend/Lillie's college roommate

Grace Anne and Lillie on their way to the awards banquet at a writers conference

A Real Joker

In spite of my medical influence over him, Jack never failed to tease me about being a graduate of the University of Texas. He kidded around a lot, and I liked that about him as I like to joke around, also.

Gabriel Ortiz, M.D.
Health Texas Medical Group, Blanco Rd.

Jack posed by the sign to remind
Lillie to keep him on a leash

Burnt Toast and Raw Eggs

Jack and Lillie came in once a week early in the morning after their shopping trip to Walmart. After they had been here several times, I recognized their car when they pulled into the parking lot, and I would get their favorite table ready. Jack was hilarious. He couldn't seem to understand anyone but Lillie. I would ask him something, and Lillie would repeat it. She didn't speak any louder or any different that I could tell, so I never figured out how he could understand her but not be able to understand anyone else.

Jack liked burnt toast and undercooked eggs. The first time he said the toast wasn't burnt enough, and Zach the cook toasted it darker. Jack ate it but he still wasn't satisfied. So the next week, Zach toasted the bread until it was black on both sides and smoking. Jack said that was perfect. He liked his eggs over easy, but he didn't want any brown on the underside of the eggs. Zach soon learned to burn Jack's toast and prepare his over easy eggs just right. Jack said this was the only place he could get toast and eggs the way he liked them.

Jack loved the Aggies, and no one better say anything good about another team. He was a lot of fun and a real sweetheart.

Brittany
Waitress at Denny's Restaurant, Bitters Road and Hwy 281

One of the Best Men

Message left in the online guestbook: One of the best men I ever knew. God bless him.

On a phone call to Lillie, Emil shared the memory of a deep sea fishing trip. The Spechts were on the trip, along with Jack and his uncle, Tom McNeil. Everyone on the boat except Jack and Tom was seasick the entire time. Emil said Jack kept offering him a pimento cheese sandwich—which would have made him sick on land, much less when he was seasick.

Emil Specht
Son of Jack's good friends Leonard and Annie Specht

Two Speeds: Fast and Faster

I have known Jack most of my life. After all, he married my sister Lillie when I was only 6 years old. I have some vague memories of them visiting us on the farm on occasion or my parents, my brothers, and I going to San Antonio to visit them. Jack was very intimidating to me with his firmness and big rough voice. I remember him cooking hamburgers on his back patio for our family.

But one of the best memories I have is of him taking me on a trip with him, Lillie, and Billy to California. We drove out and the entire trip was a blast. I thought staying in hotels and swimming in the pools was great, but visiting Disneyland and Knott's Berry Farm was awesome. He was still somewhat intimidating, but by this time I was less fearful of him.

I remember as a teenager he let me drive his purple Challenger for a short distance. It was very exciting to drive such a powerful car as a teenager. When I graduated from high school and went to San Antonio College I lived just down the street from Jack and Lillie. I spent a lot of time at their house that year, and Jack never made me feel unwelcome in any way. Later in my late 20's I went to work for Lillie in her interior landscape business. I lived with Lillie and Jack, and, once again, he made me feel welcome and never as an intrusion. By now, I had learned that Jack was all bark and no bite.

Jack had a great sense of humor and was not opposed to telling a few off-color jokes but was very selective who he told those to so as not to offend anyone.

Jack's driving: He had two speeds of driving—fast and faster. On one occasion he asked me to help him tow one of his Mazdas to his mechanic. He was driving the towing vehicle and I was driving the truck being towed. I just remember holding onto the steering wheel as we passed cars all the way around 1604. He always thought that traffic laws were meant for everyone but him.

After Jack was diagnosed with Alzheimer's, I purchased a new car. It was equipped with OnStar, and I thought that Jack would enjoy the technology. It was one of the extremely few times that I remember Jack riding in someone else's car and being a passenger. As I thought, he was tickled with the directions and the countdown to the exact foot. However I crossed the solid white line as I merged onto the expressway. Jack said very seriously, "You just broke at least ten laws crossing that line." I wanted to say "Really, Jack?," but I remained quiet.

Jack was extremely proud of being an Aggie. I have never known anyone that identified so closely to a college even fifty years after they graduated. He carried the things he learned at Texas A&M with him throughout his life.

Jack's philosophy was it is easier to ask forgiveness than to ask permission. Once when we were taking care of the plants at a Mama's restaurant in Austin, the technician was using a ladder to reach plants in planters all the way up the wall. The ladder slipped, and she fell and broke her elbow. To ensure safety Jack decided that he would drill a hole in the "foot" of the ladder and in the floor and place a large nail through the holes to hold the ladder in place. He walked into the restaurant with a drill, placed the ladder in the appropriate place, and proceeded to drill a hole in the floor. Soon enough, the manager walked in demanding to know what was going on. Jack calmly explained what he was doing. He then placed a chair leg over the hole and said, "See, you can't even see it." The manager turned and walked away, and it was never an issue.

Jack was extremely loyal. He did business with the same companies, and within those companies, the same people for years. He would wait for half an hour for the person he wanted to see even if three or four other people offered to help him in the meantime.

On the day Jack died, he turned to Lillie and said, "Let's go out for enchiladas." Jack hadn't been able to sit up, much less go out, so Lillie suggested they send me to pick up enchiladas and bring them home. Jack started putting his legs off the side of the bed and insisted he wanted to go out. Lillie said she would much rather eat at home. Finally she convinced Jack, and off I went to Taco Cabana. When I got back to the house, I mixed his next dose of Ativan in a few bites of enchilada before taking the box to Lillie in the bedroom. She fed Jack the first bite, and he said, "Oh, that's good." When she lifted the spoon with the next bite, he shook his head and kept his mouth closed. Lillie reminded him he had wanted enchiladas, and he finally ate the second bite. But when she tried to give him another bite, he asked, "Why am I eating enchiladas?" Before either of us could answer, he said, "Oh, I asked for enchiladas." He shook his head and said, "I don't want enchiladas … I want enchiladas." He refused another bite. "I don't want enchiladas," he said. "I want enchiladas." We kept trying to get him to eat a few more bites, and he kept saying, "I don't want enchiladas. I want enchiladas." I whispered to Lillie that I was ready to eat the enchiladas with the Ativan! Those two bites of enchiladas turned out to be Jack's last meal.

The only time I ever saw Jack get emotional was when he talked about his love for Lillie. He would cry telling me how much he loved her. I loved him for the way he cared for my sister.

Nancy Nicholson
Lillie's sister

Colorful, Helpful, and Knowledgeable

Jack was the most colorful, interesting man on the block. He was the most helpful, knowledgeable man I ever met. He assisted me in working on my vehicles and yard. We talked about guns, hunting, and law enforcement. He was so good to my kids, and they loved his Texas A&M boxers. Great man. Great neighbor. May God take care of this great Aggie and great neighbor.

David Gutierrez
Former neighbor

Jack and Lillie with Lillie's sister Nancy

Aggie Engineer

Jack—what can I say? He pulled into our store (Walmart #1198) late at night/early morning. As he came through, he made our night. He always had great A&M pride and would talk about his career as a top engineer. As time passed, we at the front end of #1198 became closer and closer to Jack. He was always scooting through eating his chips and wouldn't put 'em down for nothing. We all had great pleasure getting the chance to know and help Jack. He is missed dearly.

Amy, CSM
Walmart #1198, Hwy 281 @ Loop 1604

Jack in the backyard of his beloved home

Loud and In Charge

We first met Lillie and Jack Ammann in 1999 when we came to All Saints. Our history with Jack included at least one Thanksgiving, a church picnic, Lenten spaghetti suppers (events involving food seem to be a theme), and various meetings with Lillie at their house. I know Jack was the recipient of at least one Aggie-related gift from a parish bazaar, the giving of which typifies (all at once) Lillie's love and support of her husband and her parish—and Jack's love for the Aggies.

Lillie was an active parishioner and Jack was ... (more than merely) the husband of an active parishioner—a man of faith in his own right, but not one to darken the All Saints' doorstep overmuch. In this regard, as in all others, Jack was Jack. I would not be surprised to learn that there was a part of him that was just waiting for a good reason to start going back to church again. I remember him telling me that he'd come to church if I would preach a sermon about John Newton and *Amazing Grace*. I always intended to, but then my time at All Saints wrapped up more quickly than expected and I never got to take him up on his offer. I would have loved to joke with him about how well the roof seemed to be holding up (i.e., not caving in at all) and how we had some good Aggie engineers work on it so that we'd be prepared for his visit and could be sure it was safe for him to come again.

Heather and I always considered Jack a friend and wished we would have been able to see more of him. Our memories of Jack are that he was *loud and in charge*, gregarious, a center of attention whenever he was present. "He was a good looking man," (said Heather,) with sparkling blue eyes. He was friendly and intelligent, but he didn't flaunt it—he was an Aggie, after all, not some "damn Yankee!" Jack always loved a good laugh and a good story. He loved some stories so much we could almost always count on hearing one of them — always told with either the passion or good humor for which Jack was known.

I never thought of Jack as an old man, though I have since learned that he was older than I ever would have thought. Jack was young at heart. He was also a devoted husband. I learned this from hearing stories from Lillie, from observing his little acts of love and service (not to be confused with *public displays of affection*, which I do not recall), and from reading *Stroke of Luck*. Jack was, of course, the main male character. I was blessed in learning of a tender, romantic side of Jack that I didn't otherwise get to see. I wish I had kidded him about it more when I had the chance!

I remember when Jack first got his "dream job" of driving the school bus. Having driven a school bus years before, I never quite understood how that could be his dream job! However, it was something he always wanted to do, and when he finally got the chance, he did it with the same gusto and zeal that made him so successful at everything else he put his hand to. Jack Ammann must have been, without doubt, the most dedicated bus driver ever to have chauffeured the students of San Antonio! Come to think of it, I am surprised the world has not been treated to a best-selling volume of bus driving stories with Jack Ammann as author and Lillie as "ghost writer." You know the last thing a mischievous student would want to see was Jack Ammann pulling that bus over and coming down the aisle! I can picture Jack's bus being the best ordered bus in the fleet, the cleanest at the end of the day, and the one where the kids would be most likely to remember their bus driver long after they had forgotten other large parts of their school experience. I can also imagine that on Jack's bus, a child could feel safe—even if it was the only time of the day that child felt safe; and if I had to guess, I'd guess that this desire to "make a difference" was at the root of Jack's dream to be a bus driver. At some point during his long and varied experience, he got the idea that a bus driver could really make a difference for kids, and from there it became the "dream" that he eventually realized.

There's a syndicated radio station that played in San Antonio while we were there: Jack FM. It was a radio station with an attitude that seemed to fit Jack Ammann almost to a T. Their motto was a proud and flippant "Playing whatever we want" or "Playing whatever the heck we feel like playing." It was all done in a fun way that said, "We are gonna do what we want—if you like it, stay and listen; if not, go listen somewhere else." That was Jack. If he had an opinion, it was always a strong one. Take him or leave him, love him or not, Jack was Jack. He loved what and whom he loved; and he hated what (and whom!?) he hated. As for Heather and me, we loved him. We will always remember his hearty laughter, his welcoming greeting, and his stories (surely adhering to the old military standard of "at least 10% truth" for each exaggeration?!!). Most of all we will miss his ability to be there for our friend Lillie, whom we also love. We pray for you both fondly.

The Reverend Jerry Sherbourne
Chaplain (Captain), US Army
Former priest at All Saints Anglican Church

"Hi, Jack"

I remember Jack coming to the salon with Lillie. He would walk in the door, and I would say, "Hi, Jack." He always responded, "Don't say that in an airport! We'll all go to jail!"

Kathie Maroudas
Friend/Lillie's hairdresser

Jack loved to laugh at his own jokes

Never a Dull Moment

I will always remember Jack—especially his humor and outlooks on world views! After my stroke, Jack would pick me up to go to their house because I can no longer drive. One time, when I was feeling kind of weak, he came up on my driveway, onto my grass, and then drove his van right up to my front door! I loved it! And I loved him.

Another time when he picked me up, he said, "You're making progress. I see you're walking better." I was surprised he noticed, but he said, "I've been watching you like I watched Lillie after her stroke." He went on to tell me how afraid he'd been when Lillie had the stroke. He thought he might lose her. But then he decided that wasn't an option. He was going to make sure she came out of it okay. "Sometimes you need a little push to do what you have to do to get better," he said. "I could always tell when Lillie needed a push or when she had a bad day."

He seemed to have an innate ability to understand people and he appreciated mankind.

Jack would come out to Lillie's office and talk to Lillie and me. He'd have a joke for us or the latest crazy thing the politicians were doing! There was never a dull moment when Jack was around. We will all miss him terribly, but I know he is up in heaven with all of the Aggies that went before him and his little Kitty.

Blessings to you, Jack. We will meet again one day in the presence of our Lord.

Beverly Hart
Friend

Always Joking

I didn't know Jack very well, but I know he had a real good sense of humor and was always joking around. I was really impressed with the care and concern he showed for Lillie.

Barbara Lamar
Attorney/CPA

Jack was serious when he was performing his duties as a Master Peace Officer, but that didn't stop him from playing around and pretending to be an Old West gunslinger

Fast Enough to Scare

From the first time I met Jack, he was always very nice to me and made me feel welcome. I enjoyed taking Jack and Lillie out to eat, and Jack really piled on the food!

He drove so fast all the time, and he always wanted to drive whenever we went anywhere. His driving would scare me, and I was always glad to get where we were going.

Florencio Borrego
Boyfriend of Lillie's sister, Nancy Nicholson

Borrego and Nancy at
Jack's 76th birthday party

Racing

I remember drag racing on San Pedro in the Mazda.

Anthony Rippy
Friend/fellow school bus driver

Two of Jack's Mazdas - the red pickup and
"Little Yellow"

First Friends

My husband Harold and I met Jack for the first time when we moved into our first apartment in Dayton. Having a place of our own was really exciting for us as we had been living with his parents while he was in the Army. We got moved in, and when we went to hook up our washer, we discovered someone else was in our spot on our electrical hookup. So upstairs we went to see who was using our hookup. After a couple of good laughs, Jack moved his washer back to his side of the basement, and we soon became close friends with Jack and his wife Renee.

Harold and Jack loved drag racing and road racing—almost any kind of racing. We would go to Indianapolis for the time trials and the road races and the drag races. When Renee and I had enough racing, we would stay in town to go shopping or to see a movie or just hang out at the hotel. We went to see *Westside Story*, and the guys laughed at us all the way home because we cried over the movie.

Jack's pride and joy was his new Corvette, and he liked to take everyone for a ride. His trick was to put a hundred dollar bill on the dashboard and bet you couldn't get it, and he never lost the money. One of the men he worked with also had a new Corvette. They worked second shift close to where the new Interstate 75 was being built. They had a friend who was a police officer, and he would follow them as they drag raced their new Corvette down the new interstate.

We had many good times, as Jack and Renee were our first new friends after we were married.

My mother-in-law and I made homemade chili sauce each summer to use over spaghetti. Harold always called it a mess, and whenever I made spaghetti, we invited Jack and Renee down for dinner, and it was good.

We were so sorry to see them move back to Texas—we had lost our best friends, but we understood they needed to go home. As they were packing and deciding what they didn't want to take back, they decided not to take a bookcase that had been in the end of the living room. It was just boards, sanded smooth, and white bricks to hold the boards up. Jack had brought the bricks and boards from Texas when they came. I still have those bricks and boards, and also a spoon holder in the shape of an apple, which I still use today

Tears are running down my face as I write this. Harold and Jack both have gone home, but words cannot say how much they are missed every day.

Margaret Conrad
Ohio neighbor/friend of Jack and first wife Renee

Jack and his Corvette

A True Inspiration

I always used to love to hear about all the stories that Jack would tell me about his time at Frigidaire in Dayton (where I was born). He had several stories to tell, and they would always end with, "You can take the boy out of Texas but you can't take Texas out of the boy." He had told me that, besides Lillie, Texas A&M was the best thing that had ever happened to him. Jack was a true perfectionist. He would buy the best that money could buy, and then set out to make it better, whether it was cars, rifles, or what-have-you. He was a true inspiration to me.

Peter Lassen
Friend/fellow gun enthusiast/plumber

Aggie Jack

Pink Cigarettes

Jack, Jack, good ole Jack. He was so funny with his crusty humor. He always came through the front doors of Walmart, and he would have an A&M-Longhorn discussion with Charles. Then he would come on down and ask me to sell him cigarettes. As manly and gruff as he was, he smoked the pink package of cigs. I thought that was funny.

He will be missed by many of us here at 1198. We love you, too, Lillie.

Vicki
Walmart #1198, Hwy 281 @ Loop 1604

The macho hunter smoked pink cigarettes

Cruising at 100 MPH

Jack didn't take me cruising around the neighborhood unless you call going 100mph cruising. I think I was about five or maybe six. He strapped me and my girlfriend together in the front seat of the Corvette and took us out on NW Military Highway, which was out in the middle of nowhere in 1966. He took us up to 100 mph and scared us to death...god, was it fun!

I also remember Jack working with my Dad on the rifle team that they started in Shavano Park. Seems not too many other parents were interested in volunteering their time, but Jack came out to spend his evenings helping to teach someone else's kids how to shoot a rifle.

Matyi Specht Hord
Daughter of Jack's good friends Leonard and Annie Specht

Young Jack

Your Boyfriend is Calling

Jack was so dedicated to Lillie. Always my favorite story of him is his coming into Lillie's office after trying to call her there from his house phone. She hadn't answered, I think because we were there talking. When he came to the office, he said, "Your boyfriend is trying to call you." I didn't know what he meant. Lillie then said, "I think those calls were from Jack."

Jan Kilby
Friend/Lillie's writing colleague

Jack and Lillie at a convention banquent

I'm Staying Away from That Guy!

Shortly after we moved into our house, I heard someone yelling very loudly from the house at the end of the cul-de-sac. There was one house between us, and hearing that loud voice from such a distance, I said, "I'm staying away from that guy!" Later, though, I met Jack and realized I had the wrong impression of him. He was really very nice, and I liked him a lot.

Several years later, we had a block party for the residents on Mauze and the two families on Inne, which dead-ended into Mauze. The party was at the other end of the street from Jack's house, and he showed up in his constable's uniform. I asked him if he thought we were going to have such a wild party that we needed the law.

I have a lot of good memories of Jack from so many years as neighbors.

Danny (Dan) Gonzalez
Neighbor for more than 40 years

Talking and Listening

Jack always came by Sears where I worked to get his tires checked for air or to buy tires. It was nice talking to and listening to him. He will be missed.

Sean Breiten
Friend/business associate

Frank and wife Nelda with children Archer, Hunter, and Spencer and grandson Dalton

Generosity to Kid Brother

One of my favorite memories of Jack is traveling across the Western United States with Jack and Lillie when I was about fourteen years old. I was fortunate enough to be invited to accompany them on vacation. We drove in Jack's 1969 Chevrolet, and Jack could not wait to get to Nevada where there was no posted speed limit at the time. (Nevada pretty much flashed by.) We took an airplane tour of the Grand Canyon, where I lost my lunch all over the cockpit and the pilot. We saw the Painted Desert and Petrified Forest and stood in four states at once at Four Corners. Jack's generosity always impressed me, and it started by taking his wife's kid brother on vacation with them. I also credit that trip when I was a teenager with starting my love for the West and the desert that eventually got me to move to Phoenix.

Frank Nicholson
Lillie's brother

Rivalry

During an All Saints' Fall Festival, Steve and I were working out in the parking lot for the book sale. Lillie and Jack were out there. We were talking to Jack, and I had my Texas football shirt on because the game was on later that evening. Jack had his A&M shirt on, and the rivalry began.

We love you, Jack. We will miss you.

Debbie and Steve McCullough
Fellow parishioners at All Saints

Grandpa Jack and Mr. Jack

You know those people who you meet for the first time, and you feel as though you've known them your entire life? That is Mr. Jack.

In so many ways, he reminds me of my own Grandpa Jack, my daughter Kierstin's great-grandpa, who has been with The Lord for many years now.

It's that familiar warm, feisty, let's-see-what-I-can-do-to-help spirit that shines through and makes you fall in love with them instantly. They're down-home people of a simpler time, who can have you engrossed and living history with them through their detailed stories of young country life, the depression, war time, and great days gone by. I'm sure my Grandpa and Mr. Jack are having a good ol' time fellowshipping on the other side!

You know, my grandfather passed into eternity before my daughter was born, so Kierstin meeting Mr. Jack was special for me. She was able to experience someone very special in his own right, and who in many ways was like her own great-grandpa. And for that, we are truly blessed, and will forever be thankful.

Aundrea Hernandez
Friend/Lillie's graphic designer colleague in publishing

Everything Was a Joke

Mr. Ammann was always joking around. Even when he was in pain, he still kidded around with us and gave Dr. Ortiz a hard time about not being an Aggie.

Juan
Medical Assistant, Health Texas Medical Group, Blanco Rd.

Keeping the Neighborhood Safe from Varmints

We'll always remember you, Jack.

I've always loved my sleep on weekends. Still sleeping one early morning on a Saturday, I heard knocking on my door. I instantly knew it was Jack. I heard my husband David, say, "Jack, she's not a morning person." Jack said to wake me up—he had something really important to show me. So Dave came to the room to get me. I went to the door, and there was Jack with a dead squirrel. He said, "I shot him—take a look." He was so proud he was keeping our neighborhood free from varmints.

I will always remember him as a great neighbor and an honest and passionate man…and a diehard Aggie.

All my love and prayers,
Sandy Gutierrez
Former neighbor

Cars and Guns

I remember Mr. Jack when I going to barter for the green monster, the '69 Chevy. At the time he also had a couple of Mazdas with the rotary engines. He was saying nothing but good things about those two autos. He asked me if I wanted a ride in one. I said, "Ride?" Next thing I remember, he's doing 105 mph on Loop 410 in front of North Star Mall. Wow!

Another occasion we were on 281 South after he took me on another *ride*. Then a motorcycle passed us as if we were in reverse. Mr. Jack hit the light on top of the Chevy, and the chase began. Wow! If I remember, we were doing 117 mph.

At that point, I had to have that car. We bartered, and I gave Mr. Jack $1000 and a full auto machine gun. I talked to Mr. Jack about four months ago to buy back that gun, but God had other plans for Mr. Jack. Bless him!

Ricardo Duran Garza
Friend/Fellow car and gun enthusiast

All Those Keys

Jack bugged me to take "all those keys" off my key ring. I had upwards of fifteen to twenty keys on one ring. Jack said it would mess up the ignition over the years due to the weight. I said, "Phooey," and never took the keys off until the late 1990s when my Chrysler Town and Country would not start. So after fixing the car (lucky it was still under warranty), I succumbed to Jack's advice and now have my car key separate from my other keys.

Kenn Schaefer
Friend

Like A Dog with a Frisbee

Because of the difference in our ages, I didn't really see Jack often during my childhood. I was about eight or nine years old when he came to our house on Herweck for a holiday dinner. He was in the Army and wearing his uniform. He told me that before we ate, he would teach me to play baseball. It seemed like he used either a tennis ball or a golf ball. He would throw the ball, and I would run to get it—like a dog running after a Frisbee. I don't know how long we did this, but I had to sit down and rest after all that chasing after the ball.

I don't remember seeing Jack again until I was seventeen. Jack used his influence and great verbal skills to keep me out of prison.

He took me with him to North Star Dodge when he went to order his Dodge Challenger from the salesman, Cliff White. The car was an expensive one for the time—the princely sum of $4100. And that car could run. At the time, I was working at The Buggy Shop and had a souped-up Volkswagen that *hauled the mail*. Jack and I used to go out to "Little Green Valley," a place where local racers gathered to drag race. I won every race I ran in the VW, and Jack won every race he ran in the Challenger. I think the Challenger might have beat my car, but it would have been very close either way. Jack and I made a deal: we agreed never to race each other. We'd never know which car was faster, but neither of us would be beat. The cops showed up regularly, and everyone scattered. Jack and I raced out there a lot, but neither of us ever got a ticket.

David Ammann
Brother

Special People and Aggie Glasses

When Lillie and I were working on my book, Jack always came to the office and offered us something to drink. He loved to serve me something in one of his A&M glasses—he said only special people got to drink out of his Aggie glasses. He would call out to the office from inside the house to see if we needed water or anything else to drink.

Margaret Blincoe
Friend/Lillie's Client

Jack and Lillie with David and wife Cindy and family

Stocks and Driver's Ed

When I was six years old, Jackie gave me a special silver dollar and told me if I still had it on my sixteenth birthday, he would give me a hundred dollars. After years of updates letting him know that I still had it, my sixteenth birthday finally happened. He said he just didn't have a hundred dollars, so he gave me one share of General Motors stock. Thus began my adventures in the stock market.

Jackie also gave me adventures in learning to drive. I was getting ready to take driver's ed in early 1963. Jackie had just purchased one of the first Corvette Stingrays. Back in those days, the driver's ed cars were standard shifts. Our mother and I convinced Jackie to teach me to drive a standard using his Stingray. We went out to a deserted street called Louis Pasteur in the medical center. It took an extreme amount of patience on his part, something he was not known for, and about thirty minutes for me to get about fifty feet. Lesson over. The Mercury Comet that I used in driver's ed was considerably easier than that Stingray.

Carol Rabb
Jackie's baby sister

Fake Gruffness

I remember those times Jack came to our office with a *fake* gruffness that would throw those who didn't know Jack's sense of humor. They would think they were in trouble, then eventually realize he was a real sweetheart. He will be missed.

Jim Oliver
Friend/CPA

Jack and Lillie with his mother, sister Carol Rabb, her husband Sam and daughter Jenny and friend

Gentle Dictator

I had a soft spot in my heart for Jack because he reminded me of Mr. Moore, my elementary school bus driver. It surprised me a few years ago when I learned Jack actually had been a bus driver! Mr. Moore ran a tight "ship" on that bus, and yet because of it was respected and well loved. His gentle dictatorship created a safe environment where kids actually wanted to ride the bus. I always imagined Jack was very much the same as a driver. I look at all that happens on busses these days and know that none of it would happen with men like Jack and Mr. Moore at the wheel!"

Jennifer Goodman
Friend

Jack driving the school bus

What Marriage Should Be

I met Jack just a few times. The most compelling thing about him to me was his love for Lillie. To see Jack and Lillie together, to hear either speak of the other, was to see what marriage should be.

Janet Kaderli
Lillie's writer friend

Jack and Lillie on their wedding day

Family Friday Nights

I remember the times when all three of us would go to Valerio's Italian Restaurant. I think to this day they had some of the best spaghetti and meatballs on the planet. And we'd go in and get seated and the sons of the original owner who ran the restaurant would come out and be glad to see us.

Jack would let me know he knew their father when they started, and they were all great friends. They'd let us know we had a special meal coming! Then out comes these three huge bowls of spaghetti and meatballs. If you left there hungry that was your fault! Then they'd ask us if we wanted any more! NOOOOOOO! Then they'd tell us to come back again. Jack would talk to them for a few minutes and then we'd go. That was one of the good times I remember and wish were still around.

I also remember when we would go to the Hungry Farmer restaurant on Friday nights. We went so often on Friday nights that the waitress knew us. They had great steaks but used frozen fries. Sometimes before we left the house, Jack would clean and cut two pounds of potatoes into fries to take to the Hungry Farmer. Then he would put them all in a zipper plastic bag and then tell Lillie to put that obscene bag of raw fries in her purse. She would say, "It's too heavy and it's embarrassing!" But she would eventually agree to carry the potatoes inside her purse. Ha ha ha! We'd sit down, get our usual waitress, and she would come out with three salads and three large teas, take our order, and take the raw potatoes to the kitchen for the cook to fry. I would get a single serving steak and Jack would order this Brontosaurus steak that he would cut in half to share with Lillie. It was so big that sometimes Lillie would bring some of her steak home.

That was our Friday night family thing, talking and having fun, Jack being silly and telling jokes. Those are the times I miss, and I'm sure Mom does too.

Love,
William Ammann
Son

Jack and William on
William's first Christmas with Jack & Lillie

Comfortable and Happy

What a wonderful idea to write Jack's story! I remember his:

- big booming voice
- jokes
- undershorts

He was so comfortable with himself and was happy with his life and loved Lillie.

Barbara A.F. Greene
Friend/Lillie's client

Jack and the Infamous Undershorts

Scared to Death

Well, hell, Jack!

I remember meeting you twenty-eight years ago, and you scared me to death with that bold voice and even bolder personality. I soon found out that the bark was far worse than the bite, and you were just a crusty marshmallow.

Hours on end of collected stories, jokes, and looking at your cars. How does one remember so much?

Stubborn, opinionated, and very pure of heart, especially when it came to protecting Lillie. The devotion to her was so obvious.

So full of life and energy and passion. I can see you giving them hell up there to get things in order.

Rachel Taylor Hooper
Friend/business associate

Tears

Why do I mourn

You cannot feel the tears

Dripping one

By salty one

Into the chasm gouged

In my existence

My lifeblood seeping away

As surely as your own

Once did

Into the crumbling earth

And endless void

Why do I cry

If you aren't here

To feel my grief

Or comfort me

And tell me that

You understand

And share my pain

No matter how alone

I seem to be

Jack Stories

Grief has no meaning

For those whose hearts

No longer beat

Why then

These desperate sobs

That seek to cleave

My own in two?

Perhaps, in truth

They're not for you

But meant for me

Because with your death

I've lost a part of

What made me

Me

And I grieve the loss

Of the person I

Can never be

Again

Miriam Ruff
Lillie's writing colleague

A Bulldog on a Chain

During our sophomore year at Texas A&M, Jack, Bartell Zachry, and I had been hunting up on Jack's grandparents' place in Boerne. We were dirty and smelled pretty bad. Bartell's father (H.B. Zachry) had asked us to look at a car Mr. Zachry was considering as a gift for his wife. We went straight to the Cadillac dealership after our hunting trip, not bothering to change or clean up. The salesman was slow in getting up out of his chair and coming over to us. He looked us over and said he didn't think we could afford a Cadillac. Jack just exploded. "All we want to do is look at the car." The salesman asked us to leave, and Bartell got on one side of Jack, and I got on the other. We went out to Bartell's grungy Jeep and drove to the Zachry home.

When Mr. Zachry asked us what we thought of the car, we told him the salesman wouldn't let us look at it because we didn't look like we could afford it. I understand Mr. Zachry called the Cadillac dealership and let them know he didn't appreciate the treatment we got. Of course, Jack and I couldn't afford the car, and I doubt that Bartell could on his own. But Mr. Ammann could certainly afford a Cadillac; in fact, he drove a Cadillac convertible. Mr. Zachry didn't drive a Cadillac, but he could certainly afford one, and it wasn't unusual for him to give his wife expensive gifts. I always remember Jack just exploding at the salesman—he was like a bulldog on a chain.

Laland McCormick
Friend

Taking Care of Mr. Jack

I helped Mama take care of Mr. Jack. I liked to give him his medicine and put the lotion on his forehead.

Morgan Gonzales
Four-year-old daughter of caregiver Betsy Gonzales

Mr. Jack and Morgan after application
of lotion to Jack's forehead

Always in My Corner

I didn't meet my uncle until I was a grown man already. Since then, a lot of time has passed. I have so many special memories of him. His smile and laughter could fill a room, and that's what I will miss most about him. He and I, although we were never extremely close, always seemed to agree about life's struggle. He was a proud man, and he knew what his moral center was. I will never forget that he had a choice—to accept or reject me. All the years I've known him, not once did I ever feel rejected. I always felt that he was in my corner. I will always have a sense of regret for the times we never got to share together, but I know that in my heart, he has always been with me. That's just the way he made me feel, and I will always remember that the most.

Scott Hurt
Nephew

Lillie and Jack with brother David and Scott, Rachel, Zoe, and Megan Hurt

Whatever She Needs

Jack,

I will miss you my dear friend.

Two favorite memories:

1) Jack always watched out for me when I was at Lillie's office. "Lillie, did you get Shawne some water? Get her whatever she needs. And if you need me to handle those people at work for you, just let me know. I'll show you how to handle them."

2) Don't say "Hi, Jack" in the airport.

Shawne Zakaria
Friend/Lillie's client

Miss Lillie, We will be praying for you.

Iman Zakaria
Seven-year-old daughter of Shawne Zakaria

A Gentleman's Gentleman

I was Jack's barber for more than thirty years, and throughout that entire time, he always treated me with dignity and respect. He was a gentleman's gentleman. I always looked forward to his visits to the barber shop. We always kidded around with each other, and our tongue-in-cheek banter kept everyone in the shop laughing. He will always hold a special place in my heart.

Carl Simons
Friend/barber

Mr. Aggie and the Professional

I knew Jack for around 15 years. He would call me and leave me a message: "This is Jack Ammann, Mr. Aggie."

I'd go over to Jack's house to do a project, and he would have done the job in his head and tell me how he thought best to do the job. However, he would tell me, "You're the professional, so don't let me get in your way!

Jack would come out in skivvies—Aggie boxers, of course—and an A&M T-shirt. That was the standard at home.

We would go to Home Depot and he would ask to speak to the manager where he would be frank with them. The manager would "yes, sir" Jack to death, and Jack would always get his way. Then away we would go back the house to do our project.

Jack would sometimes get away in his Caddie, going down 281 doing 80 miles an hour. He would often say that he could go faster if he had fine-tuned the car.

Jack would call me once every three to four months. He was a real trip to talk to and work for. He was the epitome of an old Aggie. As an Aggie Dad, I admired that. I will forever remember the times I spent with Jack and those memories will always make me smile. So tonight, in honor of my friend, I say "Gig 'em, Jack!"

Ed Zamora
Friend/electrician

Proud to be an American

Jack Ammann was the most conservative American I ever met. He was not afraid to share his views with anyone who would listen. His TV was tuned to the Fox network 24/7. Once a phone surveyor asked what networks or local TV stations he watched. He said, "Just Fox and nothing else." The caller didn't believe him and kept asking, "Surely you must watch something on the other channels?" He said, "No, I only watch Fox."

Jack was proud to be an American, and he will be missed by all who knew him.

David Bowles
Friend/Lillie's client

Tips

Every time I went to clean house for Jack, he always had a funny joke to tell me. I cannot remember every one of them, but I remember how he always gave me advice. The first time I cleaned for him, he made sure to let me know that if he gives me a tip, he intends it for a gift, and I don't have to tell the IRS. It's just for me. I also remember that he taught that when I am parked on a hill to put my car in neutral first before I put the emergency brake on. That will keep the car from jerking when I put it back in gear. It was better for the transmission. I loved Jack. He was such a caring and wonderful man.

Bonnie Schnautz
Friend/former housekeeper

An Ambassador for the Nation of A&M

The first time Pat Davis and I went to do some work for Jack, he drove us to Home Depot to pick up some material. I think he tried to see if he could scare us with his driving, and he came close to doing that. He always wanted things done in a certain way and was very specific about what he wanted — nothing but the best. At Home Depot, he was treated like royalty and got just what he wanted. That Reader's Digest feature — My Most Unforgettable Character — could have been created for Jack. I liked him from our very first meeting, and I miss him now.

Alan Fortenberry
Friend/handyman/photographer

Aggie Glasses and Cherished Memories

What a blessing to know you, Lillie, and to have known Jack. Both of you always made me feel welcome in your home. I will miss Jack's sense of humor and hearty laugh. I will always cherish how generous he was in sharing with me his Texas Aggie glasses filled with lots of my favorite soda. I often think of the day we all sat down at your dining table eating Whataburgers. I cherish that day.

Beverly Ellison
Friend, Lillie's former assistant

A Texan in Whom Is No Guile

(Paraphrased excerpts from Father Chip's homily at the funeral service)

The last time I saw Jack was about ten days before he died. I said, "Jack, the time is coming for you to go home, and you need to pack your bags. Are you ready?"

Jack answered, "My bags are packed. I'm ready."

Each one of us will have to stand before the Lord at the end of our life. If you can't say as Jack did that your bags are packed and you're ready, talk to me. We never know when our time will come, and we need to be ready all the time.

Jack reminded me of St. Bartholomew, also called Nathanael in the Bible. You might not agree with Jack, but you always knew where he stood. Like Jack, Nathanael said exactly what he thought. When Philip told Nathanael that they had found the Messiah—Jesus of Nazareth, Nathanael answered, "Can anything good come out of Nazareth?" Philip took Nathanael to see Jesus, who greeted Nathanael by saying, "Behold an Israelite indeed, in whom is no guile!" I can hear the Lord greeting Jack in Heaven: "Behold a Texan indeed, in whom is no guile!"

The Venerable Fr. C.B. "Chip" Harper..."Father Chip"
Rector, All Saints Anglican Church
Priest/fellow Aggie

Jack and his beloved
Kitty

Jack and his mother,
Louise Carson, on
the occasion of her
85th birthday

Jack and Lillie with his family on the occasion of his grandmother's 100th birthday:
Lillie, Jack, Old Mama (grandmother), Jenny Rabb (niece), Aileen Mangham (aunt), Louise Carson (mother), Carol Rabb (sister), Charles Mangham (uncle), Scott Rabb (nephew)

Lillie's Jack Stories

Favorite Stories from Jack's Wife

Some of these stories have been taken from Lillie's blog.
Others have been written specifically for this book.

"...And they shall become one flesh."

Jack always said the he and I complemented each other. He was strong in math and science, and I am strong in English and writing. Jack had good eyesight and poor hearing, and I have poor eyesight and good hearing. Jack was outgoing and colorful—everyone who met him remembered him; I tend to be quieter and to stay more in the background. Together, Jack said, we could do anything. We were two halves of one whole.

As the Bible says, "Therefore a man shall leave his father and his mother and hold fast to his wife, and they shall become one flesh." ~ Genesis 2:24, ESV

Jack was more than thirteen years older than me. During premarital counseling, the priest pointed out repeatedly that I would probably have to take care of him in his old age. I agreed that might happen, but I was willing to do it.

As it turned out, I had a stroke at age 45, and Jack had to care for me for months during my recovery. He would do anything I really needed, but if he thought I could do something—even if it would be hard—he insisted I do it myself. Although I didn't like it at the time, I know now I wouldn't have recovered nearly as well if he hadn't pushed me to do more than I thought I could. He was always confident I would recover. When I had moments of weakness and doubt, he told me there was no reason to worry because I was going to be fine.

Twenty years later, the situations were reversed, and Jack was the one in need of care. I was so blessed to be able to care for him at home. I have wonderfully patient clients who understood that Jack came first, and I have a great assistant who took over important projects and finished what I couldn't do. For the last couple of years of Jack's life, I spent a great deal of time with him, and I was always available if he needed me or if he simply wanted my company. For the last few months, I was with him constantly and cared for him with the help of a wonderful caregiver. There were challenging times, but thanks be to God, I have loving family, friends, and church family to support me.

Some of the most precious times Jack and I spent together were in those last months. We would sit on the front porch, and Jack would often turn to me and say, "We have a really good life, don't we?" And we did—a wonderful life, indeed.

Jack had seen my father with Alzheimer's forget my mother, and he worried his dementia would progress to the point that he might not know me. He would come to my office, open the door, and say, "No matter what happens, I want you to always remember I'll always love you." Praise God, he knew me to the end.

About a week before he died, we were in a nursing home while arrangements were made to accommodate his needs at home and to provide constant care since I couldn't care for him alone. Jack never knew he was in a nursing home—he thought he was still in a hospital. We had a private room, and I stayed in the room with him. One morning I was in the bathroom getting dressed, and I heard him talking to a nurse. She said, "Your wife sure takes good care of you." He said, "Yes, she does. We both meant it when we said, 'for better for worse, for richer for poorer, in sickness and in health, to love and to cherish, till death us do part.'" He repeated those exact words at a time when he couldn't carry on a conversation. He couldn't remember what happened five minutes before, but he remembered our wedding vows from more than forty-five years ago.

Jack's Generous Nature

Jack had such a generous nature that he would do things for people and never even mention them to me. One day I was reading Paul Thompson's column in the San Antonio Light (obviously a very long time ago!). The column was about a phone call Thompson had received from a reader who was new to San Antonio. The man had tried to pay for his groceries with an out-of-state check, but HEB wouldn't accept it. The newcomer said he would have to put the groceries back because he didn't have a credit card or enough cash with him to pay for what he bought. The man in line behind him tapped him on the shoulder and said, "Write me a check, and I'll pay for your groceries." He asked the checker for the amount and handed her the money. The man who was new to Texas asked how to make out the check. The kind and trusting man behind him gave his name: Jack Ammann.

This is but one example of many times Jack helped someone in need, whether he knew them or not. When we owned the interior landscape company, Jack handled the accounts payable and receivable. The employees quickly learned to go to Jack first if they wanted a pay advance or some special concession. He always helped them out—advancing money, loaning them a vehicle if they had car trouble, or whatever else they might need.

One time I got very upset with him for loaning an employee money. The young man had come to me and asked to borrow money to pay for an abortion for his girlfriend. I told him we would not do anything to make an abortion possible and encouraged him to reconsider. However, when Jack came to the shop, the worker met him in the parking lot and asked him for a loan—not saying what it was for. Jack wrote him a check before I had a chance to talk to him. He wouldn't have knowingly aided an abortion, but he was so trusting that when an employee said he needed money for a family emergency, Jack gave it to him with no questions asked.

My sister Nancy's boyfriend, Florencio Borrego (known to all as Borrego), speaks very little English. After my mother died, we didn't have family holidays at the farm anymore. So Jack and I invited Nancy and Borrego to have Thanksgiving dinner with us at Luby's. Jack asked me to type up a special Thanksgiving blessing he wanted to say. Then he had me copy and paste the text into Google Translate and get a Spanish translation. We printed the prayer in both English and Spanish so Borrego would not feel left out.

Happy 40ᵗʰ Anniversary to Us

Posted on Lillie's blog May 31, 2007

Not very long ago, so it seems, I thought anyone forty years old was ancient. All of sudden, I'm way past forty years old – my husband and I have been married for forty years today.

Jack and I met when I got a summer job during college in the same office at Kelly Air Force Base where Jack worked as a civilian industrial engineer. I started that job on my twentieth birthday, and Jack followed the boss and me around when the boss introduced me to other employees. Jack teased me that the name plates would be removed from all the desks the next day, and I would have to remember everyone's name. It wasn't particularly funny, but he laughed at his own joke so much that I had to laugh along with him.

A little more than two months later on a visit to Jack's home a few days before my job ended, we sat on his couch as I told him my future plans. After I talked about returning to college, getting my degree, finding a job after graduation ... he looked at me and said, "When are you going to marry me?"

I responded, "When are you going to ask me?"

He asked, and I accepted.

My father was worried that this older "city slicker" was out to take advantage of a naive, young country girl. The priest who gave us premarital counseling warned me I had to be prepared to take care of Jack in his old age since he's more than thirteen years older than I am.

Daddy's worries soon disappeared as he came to adore Jack. Daddy barely had a high school education back in the days of eleven-year schools, and he lived on the same farm from his birth to his death. Jack has a Master of Science degree in

Systems Management Engineering and has always lived in the city of San Antonio. However, they were far more alike than it appeared on the surface – both highly intelligent, deeply caring men with great senses of humor. I think my mother recognized that right away. She liked Jack from the beginning and grew to love him as quickly as my father did.

And as for the priest's warning that I would have to take care of Jack in his old age ... I was the one who had a stroke after we'd been married for twenty-five years. Jack is the one who cared for me during the many months of my recovery and continues to take care of me as I experience recurring health issues. Though he has had medical challenges of his own in recent years, I've been far more dependent on him than vice-versa.

When Jack's mother was alive, she used to tell me I deserved a gold star for putting up with him so long. He is impatient, often short-tempered, always opinionated. He could give a much longer list of my faults, but I'll leave that to him. On the other hand, he is trustworthy, dependable, generous, caring, smart, unselfish, and funny. We laugh – a lot! We love each other very much, and we both love the Lord.

Love, laughter, and faith have made forty years fly by. I wish you the same joy and blessings that we have experienced for forty years ... and that we plan to experience for many more!

What I Learned from a Colorful Character: Eliminate This Word

Posted on Lillie's blog March 4, 2010

This blog post is my entry into two online events: Words Matter Week: What Word Would You Eliminate? and What I Learned from a Colorful Character group writing project.

You see, I've been married to a colorful character for nearly 43 years. I've laughed every day, and I haven't been bored a single minute. Jack is smart, funny, opinionated, assertive, upbeat, tenacious, independent, determined, self-confident, perfectionistic, and unconventional.

Recently, all the waitresses in the restaurant gathered around the cash register to listen to Jack's silly banter as he paid for our meal. One of them said, "Y'all have to come back more often to entertain us and keep us from getting bored."

This week, the election worker who set up the voting machines for us told Jack, "Hey, I remember you from the last election. Glad to see you again."

Whether we're at the bank, the grocery store, or the dry cleaners—if Jack has been there before, someone remembers him and smiles.

When I had a stroke, he took care of me and did all the things I couldn't do for myself. More importantly, he had the attitude that recovery was the only option. Regardless of what it took, it was just a matter of time before I would be well again. "The improbable can be done immediately," he said. "But the impossible takes just a little bit longer."

If I ever say, "I can't," he responds, "Eliminate that word from your vocabulary!"

Jack Stories

At age 77, he's slowing down a little, but the word can't still isn't in his vocabulary, which brings me to Words Matter Week's Blog Challenge. Each day of the week, the Words Matter blog posts a question and encourages readers to post the response to the question on their own blog. Today's question is this:

If you had to eliminate one word or phrase from the English language, what would it be? Why?

Jack, my colorful character, taught me the answer to that question, both by words and actions.

I would eliminate the word cannot (can't) because we are all capable of far more than we give ourselves credit for, and we tend to accomplish what we expect to accomplish. As Henry Ford said, "If you think you can do a thing or think you can't do a thing, you're right."

Thanks to Jack, I've accomplished far more than I ever expected. Most of all, I've enjoyed the journey filled with love and laughter.

Happy 44ᵗʰ Anniversary to Us

Posted on Lillie's blog May 31, 2011

Forty-four years ago I walked down an improvised aisle on my parents' enclosed back porch to meet my groom, my hero, my colorful character—Jack.

We've faced a few challenges in our lives, and each of us has cared for the other during illnesses. However, we've never lacked for love or laughter.

Today we carry more pounds and wrinkles, and we move a little slower. Some of our laughs today come from what Jack thinks I or someone else said, which is often very different from what was actually said. His hearing is poor, and he says he's filled his brain up in seventy-eight years of living so he doesn't have room for more. So sometimes his misunderstandings are pretty funny.

Jack used to do all the grocery shopping and the laundry. Now, the laundry is my job, and we share the shopping. Our trip to Walmart at 2 AM is a highlight of our week. I've always been a night owl, and Jack sleeps off and on through the day and night, so the middle of the night is a great time for us. We don't do well in crowds, so we enjoy shopping when there are few customers around.

But what makes our shopping so special are the people at our local Walmart. Jack used to shop at a local grocery store, and we ended up at Walmart the first time because it happened to be close by on my way home from an emergency room visit. I was having myoclonic seizures in the car while Jack went in to get a prescription filled, and four Walmart managers came out to the car and stayed with me, comforting me the entire time. So Jack started shopping there and got acquainted with the store general manager, Al Slavin, a fellow Texas Aggie.

Jack Stories

After shopping became too difficult for Jack to manage on his own, we started our wee-hours-of-the-morning shopping schedule. We realized the store would be full of stockers replenishing the shelves, and we knew we could ask questions if we needed help. But we didn't know how helpful and friendly the staff would be. I would love to name each one individually, but I don't even know all their names.

Both of us use the store scooters, and everywhere we go in the store, workers ask if we need help. If we happen to arrive when some of the stockers are taking a break in front of the store, a couple will go get scooters and bring them out to us. The guys cleaning the floor stop to greet us and ask how we are. The checkers and managers joke with us and go out of their way to be helpful. I never enjoyed shopping before, but now Jack and I both look forward to our Walmart outing.

After we finish shopping, we head off to breakfast at Denny's at San Pedro and Bitters. Brittany sees us pulling into the parking lot, and she has our table ready and my decaf brewing. She's always upbeat and enthusiastic and remembers what we like.

If anyone had told me forty-four years ago that we would look forward to a weekly date of grocery shopping and breakfast, I wouldn't have believed it. But anything I do with Jack is fun, and the people at Walmart and Denny's make our date even better!

Jack has a doctor's appointment today, then we'll have lunch at Mr. and Mrs. G's Home Cooking, a little hole-in-the-wall cafeteria-style restaurant that has the best Southern home cooking you can imagine.

Happy anniversary, Jack. I love you!

Happy 79th Birthday to Jack

Posted on Lillie's blog January 3, 2012

Today is my husband Jack's 79th birthday. This picture with his sister Carol and brother David was taken at his 76th birthday party, and he still looks the same. He has a few health problems and has slowed down some, but he's still just as fun-loving as ever with a fantastic sense of humor.

Sometimes he remembers things from the distant past more readily than current events. We spend a lot of time just sitting on the front porch talking. He enjoys telling stories of favorite things that have happened in his life.

He was the highest paid engineer in his graduating class from Texas A&M—by $1.67 a month. In 1960, he made a whopping $551.67 per month! He had interviewed with three companies and been offered a job by all of them. He chose Frigidaire Division of General Motors in Dayton, Ohio.

Jack also earned another distinction at General Motors—he was responsible for the firing of the only union employee to be fired in a long period of time. The employee accosted Jack one day complaining about something, and in their encounter, the employee grabbed Jack's tie and pulled Jack toward him. Although management was hesitant to take on the union to fire one of its members, everyone agreed that was an assault that couldn't be tolerated. Jack went through the lengthy process, until finally one day, three burly armed security guards showed up at the assembly line and escorted the employee outside the plant with orders never to return.

Although he really liked his job and his bosses really liked him, Jack finally decided that "you can take the boy out of Texas, but you can't take Texas out of the boy." He took a job at Kelly Air Force Base in San Antonio and moved back to Texas.

Jack Stories

A couple of years after Jack went to work at Kelly, I got a summer job in his office. Jack often says—and I agree completely—that divine intervention led him to move from Ohio to Texas!

At first, my father didn't approve. Jack was nearly fourteen years older than I was, and he had been divorced. Worst of all, he was a city slicker, and my father was convinced he was going to take advantage of this little country hick. However, it didn't take long for Daddy to come to love Jack like a son. Mama had loved him from the first time she met him.

I returned to Georgetown, Texas, for my final year at Southwestern University. Because of advanced placement in several courses and taking 20 hours per semester, I lacked only one course to graduate after three years. We were married on May 31, 1967, a few days after I finished school. That summer I attended a local community college and took the first and second semesters of American history simultaneously, but I had to wait until the following spring to graduate as Southwestern had only one graduation each year.

We've been married for more than 44 years and are more in love than ever.

Happy birthday, Jack!

A "Good Samaritan" Moment

Posted on Lillie's blog April 12, 2012

Recently, Jack and I were out running errands. On the way home from the post office, Jack said, "Does he need help?" I hadn't been paying attention and didn't know what he was talking about. Jack backed up a few feet to the entrance to the parking lot of a restaurant not yet open for the day. There on the sidewalk lay a young man with his wheelchair overturned beside him. He had tipped over going up the steep incline and fallen out of his chair. Fortunately, he wasn't injured, but he was helpless to get back into the chair.

Jack and I got out of the van, righted the wheelchair, and tried to lift the man back into the chair. Although he was light and both of us are large, neither of us is strong and both of us are unsteady on our feet. I had to lean against the van to keep myself upright, and between the two of us we couldn't lift the man.

Fortunately a young woman walked up, taking the same shortcut through the parking lot that the fallen man had taken. With her help, we lifted him back into his chair and checked again to make sure he wasn't hurt. The young woman pushed his wheelchair across the parking lot and to the convenience store where each had been headed before our encounter. We drove to the store and made sure the young man purchased his soda and started home safely.

We read the story of the Good Samaritan in the Bible and wonder if we would stop to help or cross by on the other side. The man we helped hadn't been attacked by robbers. He wasn't injured, and we didn't have to take him to an inn to care for him. But I hope he thought of us and the young lady who helped him up as his Good Samaritans.

Jack Stories

Often we think we have to do something large and important in order to make a difference in the world. But sometimes we are called to make just a small difference in the life of one person. And it's easy to overlook those opportunities.

I remember an incident from long ago. We had a small fire in the back seat of our car on a busy highway. Jack pulled to the side of the road, and we had to remove the back seat to put out the fire. Cars whizzed past at the speed limit (or faster), but no one even glanced our direction. We were able to get the fire out and the seat back in the car, but it would have been easier if someone had helped us.

When we were out running errands, I wasn't paying attention to my surroundings, and we would not have helped this young man if Jack hadn't noticed him lying on the sidewalk. I'm going to keep my eyes open now. Who knows what opportunities I've missed by not paying attention?

Final Words

Jack Jordan Ammann, Jr.

January 3, 1933 – September 23, 2012

Jack Jordan Ammann, Jr. entered the undiluted Presence of the Lord on September 23, 2012.

He was born January 3, 1933, to Jack Jordan Ammann and Louise Mangham Ammann (Carson). He loved to tell people he was born at the insane asylum. His grandparents worked at the San Antonio State Hospital, known as the insane asylum in the days before political correctness. His mother went into labor while visiting her parents, and the hospital doctor delivered Jack in the state hospital.

As a young boy during World War II, Jackie (as he was known) pulled his little red wagon through the neighborhood collecting scrap metal and delivering it to the fire station, setting the tone for a lifetime of passionate patriotism. Jack graduated from Texas Military Institute and entered A&M College of Texas (now Texas A&M University). After four years of college, he was classified as 1A by the draft board. Even though he was taking a five-year course, the draft board only exempted men from the draft for four years of college. He joined the Army as a volunteer rather than wait to be drafted so he could choose his field of work – stereoscopic map compiling. After completing training, he was stationed at the Presidio of San Francisco for a year, where he served as a lay reader at the Episcopal Cathedral. While stationed in Heidelberg, Germany, he spent two months touring Europe. He returned to Texas A&M after discharge from the Army and earned a Bachelor of Science degree in Industrial Engineering.

Upon graduation, he was hired by Frigidaire Division of General Motors in Dayton, Ohio. He was very proud of the fact that he was the highest-paid engineer in his graduating class with a salary that was $1.67 more than the second highest-paid graduate. At Frigidaire, the section he led held the highest efficiency rating within General Motors.

After three years, he decided "you can take the boy out of Texas, but you can't take Texas out of the boy." He left the cold and snow of Ohio to return to San Antonio as an industrial engineer at Kelly Air Force Base. He was part of a small group of engineers from around the country who created a storage manual for the entire Air Force. Later, he was the project engineer for the overhaul of the C-5 engine. He received numerous letters of commendation and certificates of achievement throughout his Civil Service career. As the representative of management in labor disputes, he never lost a case. During this time, Jack became a ham radio operator and loved talking to hams around the world, especially when he had the opportunity to relay messages during crises when no other form of communication was available.

While working at Kelly, he met the love of his life, his soul-mate, Lillian Ann Nicholson. She had a summer job in his department, and when the boss was introducing her to the staff, Jack said, "Tomorrow we're going to remove all the nameplates from the desks, and you'll have to remember all the names." He laughed uproariously at his own joke. Lillian didn't think the joke was funny, but she was captivated by his ability to enjoy his own joke so much. Jack's sense of humor always drew people to him, and he "loved a guy (or gal) with a sense of humor." At the end of the summer as she prepared to return to college, Lillian was telling Jack all her future plans. He said, "When are you going to marry me?" She answered "When are you going to ask me?" He asked, and she answered yes. They married a year later when Lillian finished her education. Soon Lillian became Lillie as Jack so affectionately called her.

Jack returned to school part-time and with Lillie's help in writing papers, he earned a Master of Science degree in Systems Management. Jack and Lillie adopted their son, William, at age eleven. When Jack retired from Kelly, he enjoyed a number of hobbies and helped Lillie in her plant business. After Lillie was robbed in her retail store, he entered law enforcement and served as a lieutenant in the Bexar County Precinct 2 Constable's Department for a number of years, achieving the status of Master Peace Officer.

After his second retirement, he realized a life-long dream of driving a bus and worked as a school bus driver. Although he was a strict disciplinarian, the children loved him. Throughout their 45 years of marriage, Jack supported Lillie in everything she did. He was her biggest cheerleader and always believed she could do anything. When she had a stroke, he took care of her and did all the things she couldn't do for herself. More importantly, he had the attitude that recovery was the only option. Regardless of what it took, it was just a matter of time before she would be well again.

A life-long avid Texas Aggie who "bled maroon," Jack had a persuasive charm that ensured he always got what he wanted and convinced everyone else they wanted it, too. Jack was a member of All Saints Anglican Church and recognized God's guidance throughout his life. After he was diagnosed with dementia, Jack sometimes got words confused and talked about God's "interference." Whatever word he used, he recognized God's guidance. A dedicated husband, a loyal friend, and a patriotic American, Jack was smart, funny, opinionated, assertive, upbeat, generous, tenacious, independent, determined, self-confident, perfectionistic, and unconventional.

He is survived by his loving and beloved wife, Lillian Ann Nicholson (Lillie) Ammann; son and daughter-in-law, William and Kathy Ammann of Kemp, Oklahoma; sister and brother-in-law, Carol and Sam Rabb of San Antonio, Texas; brother and sister-in-law, David and Cindy Ammann of Bandera, Texas; sister-in-law, Nancy Nicholson of Dilley, Texas; numerous sisters-in-law, brothers-in-law, nieces and nephews; and caregiver and surrogate granddaughter, Betsy Gonzales.